Instant Pot Crazy

Dessert Edition

Instant Pot Cookbook

INSTANT POT
Crazy

dessert edition
instant pot cookbook

Harper McKinney

BEFORE YOU BEGIN: FREE COOKBOOKS

If, like me, you are a huge cookbook addict then I'd love to help satiate your appetite for new recipes! As a small token of thanks for picking up this book I'd like to offer you the chance to pick up more just like it for free by joining my cookbook addicts club!

• Find your link at the back of this book to join the club! •

TABLE OF CONTENTS

Before You Begin: Free Cookbooks v

Introduction 1

Desserts 3

Choc Chip Honey Cake (Vegetarian) 4

Vanilla Nut Cheesecake (Vegetarian) 5

Greek Pumpkin Cake (Vegetarian) 6

Woodsy Applesauce (Vegan) 7

Mason Lemon Cheesecake (Vegetarian) 8

Chocolate Vanilla Cake (Vegetarian) 9

Creamy Almond Pudding (Vegan) 10

Apple Bread Pudding (Vegetarian) 11

Chocolate Chip Cake (Vegetarian) 12

Festive Nutty Carrot Cake (Vegetarian) 13

Pina Colada Pudding (Vegetarian) 14

Halloween Sticky Pudding (Vegetarian) 15

Maple Stuffed Peaches (Vegetarian) 16

Steamed Lime Bread (Vegetarian) 17

Festive Sweet Buttermilk Cake (Vegetarian) 18

Toothy-Fruity Cake (Vegetarian) 19

Cardamom Pear Cake (Vegetarian) 20

Lemongrass Pudding (Vegetarian) 21

Buttermilk Banana Bake (Vegetarian) 22

Bacon Pudding 23

Classic Coconut Pudding (Vegan) 24

Cherry Pie (Vegetarian) 25

Sticky Caramel Cake (Vegetarian) 26

Vanilla Butterscotch (Vegetarian) 27

Classic Messy Coconut Cake (Vegetarian) 28

Apple Peach Cobbler (Vegetarian) 29

Caramel Macchiato Cake (Vegetarian) 30

Lemon Cheesecake (Vegan) 31

Turtle Pull-Apart Biscuits (Vegetarian) 32

Chocolate Fudge Cake (Vegan) 33

General Cooking Times **35**
Beans, Legumes & Lentils.. 36
Meat & Poultry... 38
Seafood & Fish 40
Fresh & Frozen Veg 41
Rice & Grains 45
Fruits.. 47

Measurement Conversions.. **49**
Liquids, Herbs & Spices.. 50
Weights 51
Common Non-Liquids by Weight....................................... 52

Bonus: Get Free Cookbooks Like This One.................... **53**
Like This Book?... 54

INTRODUCTION

Pressure cookers have evolved so much over the years, from basic lumps of tin hidden away at the back of the cupboards to fancy, flashing hunks of brushed steel that take pride of place on the kitchen counter.

With the electric revolution has come a whole new world of possibility so that, now, anyone can produce perfectly cooked breakfasts, lunches, dinners and desserts with the push of a button, all with one piece of kit.

If you haven't picked up an Instant Pot yet, you can check out the latest and greatest version here:

• **Visit http://geni.us/instantpot to see it on Amazon!** •

This version connects to your phone – yes, seriously – to make cooking even more of a breeze. Once you've got one of these little beauties in your kitchen, you're ready to roll!

Instant Pot do a great job of providing instructions on how to use the thing, so I'm not going to waste your time going over old ground, though you will find some useful tips at the back of this book. If you're not one of those people who keeps instruction manuals (i.e. a man!) then you can find them on the Instant Pot website. Then again, if you're a man, you're probably just going to figure it out through trial and error anyway.

This cookbook is part of my *Instant Pot Crazy* series and contains something for everyone. From quick and easy meals for busy singletons, to feasts for fussy families and everything in-between; there's enough choice to put a smile on every face!

You'll find plenty of carnivorous dishes, plus generous helpings of vegetarian and vegan options. For simplicity, eggs and dairy are included in some vegetarian meals as I'm not sure whether you're lacto, ovo or something else.

This book may be small, but it's packed with a whole month of delicious dessert choices to make your evenings complete. So now you can top off mealtimes with ease! If you like what you taste, just search my name on Amazon to see the rest of the *Instant Pot Crazy* series and enjoy breakfasts, lunches and dinners made simple too!

Why no pics? It seems like we are becoming increasingly obsessed with how food looks and forgetting all about the most important aspect: the joy of improvisation and discovering new flavors for yourself.

The recipes in this cookbook are designed to enter your mouth, not a modeling contest, so I've deliberately done away with photos and made the recipes as simple to create as possible.

Cooking shouldn't cause anxiety about whether you've "done it right", so I've done my best to take that barrier away and make cooking fun and accessible for everyone. There really is no right or wrong way, only the joy of giving it a go.

As I've found out over many years of cooking, perfection does not exist. I don't hold myself to Instagram standards, I don't measure every grain of rice to the nearest 100th of a gram and, shock horror, I may even make a typo once in a while! But what it all adds up to is something that you can truly call your own.

Some of the most marvelous meals I've ever had have been a little bit rough around the edges, or even had that downright 'dropped from a rooftop' vibe going on. Others, somehow, have turned out like works of art. I encourage you to let out your inner chef and enjoy every second.

So without further ado, go forth and dive into the wonderful world of possibilities at your fingertips. We'll start with some beautiful breakfasts!

P.S. I'd love to hear about your favorite recipes, so feel free to head on over to Amazon and leave a quick review, I read every single one!

DESSERTS

CHOC CHIP HONEY CAKE (VEGETARIAN)

Not many people know this, but honey makes a drastic change when added to a cake—specifically, it makes it even more succulent. After testing it out here, you will find yourself using honey more and more often in your baking.

Serves: 6 | Prep Time: 10 mins | Cooking Time: 25 mins

INGREDIENTS

- 1 ½ cups of purpose flour
- 2 ripe bananas, mashed
- ½ cup of milk
- ⅓ cup of chocolate chips
- ¼ cup of honey
- 2 eggs
- 3 tablespoons of coconut milk
- 1 tablespoon of vinegar
- 2 teaspoons of baking soda
- 1 teaspoon of vanilla extract
- ½ teaspoon of cinnamon
- Salt

DIRECTIONS

1. Stir the milk and vinegar in a small bowl and set it aside until it curdles and becomes like buttermilk.
2. Transfer the milk mix to a food processor with the honey, banana, eggs, oil, cinnamon and a pinch of salt, then blend until smooth.
3. Add the baking soda with purpose flour and blend again.
4. Transfer the batter to a mixing bowl and fold in the chocolate chips.
5. Pour ⅔ cup of water into an Instant Pot, then place a trivet into it.
6. Pour the cake batter into a greased cake pan, then place it on the trivet.
7. Put on the lid and cook for 25 min on high pressure.
8. Once the time is up, use the quick method to release the pressure.
9. Remove the cake from the pot and allow to completely cool.
10. Serve your cake and enjoy.
    Some vanilla ice cream is perfect to serve with this cake.

Vanilla Nut Cheesecake (Vegetarian)

Sure, this is a dessert, but I won't tell anyone if you have these little beauties for breakfast, too. Always make more than you need!

Serves: 6 to 8 | Prep Time: 10 mins | Cooking Time: 18 mins

Ingredients

- 16 ounces of cream cheese
- ½ cup of sugar
- 2 eggs
- 2 tablespoons of peanut butter, powdered
- 1 tablespoon of cocoa powder
- 1 teaspoon of vanilla extract

Directions

1. Combine the eggs and cream cheese in a food processor, and blend until smooth.
2. Add the cocoa powder, peanut butter, vanilla and sugar, then blend until smooth again.
3. Spoon the mix into 6-8 mason jars.
4. Pour 1 cup of water into an Instant Pot, then place a trivet into it.
5. Place the mason jars into your cooker, then put on the lid and cook for 18 min on high pressure. (You might need to do more than one batch.)
6. Once the time is up, use the quick method to release the pressure.
7. Refrigerate for 4 hours or overnight.
8. Serve your cheesecake jars and enjoy.

Serve your cheesecake jars with some whipped cream and a sprinkle of grated chocolate.

GREEK PUMPKIN CAKE (VEGETARIAN)

Pumpkins aren't just for Halloween! Enjoy this delicious dessert with friends and family any time of year.

Serves: 6 | Prep Time: 10 mins | Cooking Time: 35 mins

INGREDIENTS

- 7 ½ ounces of pumpkin purée
- ¾ cup of purpose flour
- ¾ cup of whole wheat flour
- ¾ cup of sugar
- 2/3 cup of semi sweet chocolate chips
- 1 banana, mashed
- ½ cup of Greek yogurt
- 1 egg
- 2 tablespoons of coconut oil
- 1 teaspoon of baking soda
- ¾ teaspoon of pumpkin pie spice
- ½ teaspoon of baking powder
- ½ teaspoon of vanilla extract
- Salt

DIRECTIONS

1. Mix the baking soda and powder with purpose flour, wheat flour, pumpkin pie spice and a pinch of salt in a large mixing bowl.
2. Mix the sugar, banana, eggs, pumpkin purée, yogurt and vanilla extract in a mixing bowl, then beat with a hand mixer until smooth.
3. Add the flour mix into the banana mix and whisk until no lumpiness remains.
4. Fold in the chocolate chips, then pour the batter into a greased baking dish.
5. Pour 1 ½ cups of water into an Instant Pot, and place a trivet into it.
6. Place the cake pan on the trivet, and put on the lid. Cook the cake for 35 min on high pressure.
7. Once the time is up, use the natural method to release the pressure for 10 min, then remove the lid.
8. Allow the cake to cool down completely then serve and enjoy.

To make the cake even better, coat with some melted dark chocolate and serve with whipping cream.

WOODSY APPLESAUCE (VEGAN)

Applesauce is one of the easiest sauces ever, and you can use it for all sorts of things. However, it is easiest to prepare when you make it in an Instant Pot, taking less than 8 minutes.

Serves: 6 | Prep Time: 6 mins | Cooking Time: 8 mins

INGREDIENTS

- 8 large Granny Smith apples, peeled and chopped
- 1 cup of water
- 1 teaspoon of cinnamon powder

DIRECTIONS

1. Combine all the ingredients in an Instant Pot.
2. Put on the lid and cook for 8 min on high pressure.
3. Once the time is up, use the natural method to release the pressure for 3 min, then remove the lid.
4. Discard the water that rises to the top, then transfer to a food processor and blend until smooth.
5. Serve your applesauce and enjoy.

   A pinch of nutmeg powder will bring the best out of your applesauce.

MASON LEMON CHEESECAKE (VEGETARIAN)

This super simple cheesecake is a staple at our house and always disappears just as quickly as it was made!

Serves: 6 | Prep Time: 10 mins | Cooking Time: 8 mins

INGREDIENTS

- 16 ounces of cream cheese
- 1 jar of lemon curd
- ½ cup of granulated sugar
- ¼ cup of sour cream
- 3 eggs
- The zest of 1 lemon, grated
- 1 tablespoon of lemon juice
- 1 teaspoon of flour
- ½ teaspoon of vanilla extract

DIRECTIONS

1. Beat the cream cheese, flour and sugar until smooth.
2. Beat the lemon zest and juice, sour cream, and vanilla in another mixing bowl until creamy.
3. While slowly adding the eggs, beat constantly until smooth.
4. Gently fold in the cream cheese until the mix is smooth to make the cheesecake batter.
5. Spoon half of the batter into 6 ½-pint mason jars, then spread onto each one of them 1 tablespoon of lemon curd.
6. Spread the remaining cheesecake batter on top, then top the batter with 1 tablespoon of lemon curd per each jar.
7. Pour 1 ½ cups of water into an Instant Pot, and place a trivet into it. Place the mason jars on top.
8. Put on the lid and cook the cheesecake jars for 8 min on high pressure.
9. Once the time is up, use the natural method to release the pressure.
10. Refrigerate the cheesecake jars for 4 hours or overnight, then serve and enjoy.

    Serve your cheesecake jars with some whipped cream and chopped nuts.

CHOCOLATE VANILLA CAKE (VEGETARIAN)

Chocolate and vanilla are two flavors that everybody loves, so when you combine the two of them in a single cake, imagine the party that is going to take place in your Instant Pot!

Serves: 6 | Prep Time: 12 mins | Cooking Time: 35 mins

INGREDIENTS

- 1 ½ cups of powdered sugar
- ¾ cup of cocoa powder
- ¾ cup of purpose flour
- ½ cup of butter
- 3 egg yolks
- 3 egg whites
- 1 teaspoon of baking powder
- ½ teaspoon of vanilla extract
- Salt

DIRECTIONS

1. Beat the egg whites in a large mixing bowl until they form stiff peaks.
2. Mix the flour, cocoa powder, baking powder and a pinch of salt in another mixing bowl, then set aside.
3. Beat the egg yolks in another mixing bowl until pale.
4. Beat the butter and sugar in a large mixing bowl until light.
5. Add the egg white mix, gradually followed by the egg yolks, flour mix and vanilla extract, mixing constantly, until no lumpiness remains.
6. Pour the batter into a greased baking pan.
7. Pour 1 ½ cups of water into an Instant Pot then place a trivet into it.
8. Place the cake pan on the trivet, then put on the lid and cook for 35 min on high pressure.
9. Once the time is up, use the natural method to release the pressure.
10. Remove the cake from the pot and allow it to cool down completely the serve it and enjoy.

Drizzle some melted chocolate over the cake then serve with some vanilla ice cream and enjoy.

CREAMY ALMOND PUDDING (VEGAN)

Not many people realize that rice can be served as a dessert, but once they give it a try it often becomes a firm favorite.

Serves: 2 to 3 | Prep Time: 10 mins | Cooking Time: 4 mins

INGREDIENTS

- 2 cans of vegan condensed milk, sweetened
- 3 cups of coconut milk
- 2 cups of almond milk
- 1 cup of aborio rice
- 1 cup of water
- 3 cinnamon sticks
- 3 strips of orange zest
- 1 vanilla bean
- ½ teaspoon of ground cloves
- Salt

DIRECTIONS

1. Stir the almonds, coconut milk and water into an Instant Pot.
2. Press the sauté button on the pot, then bring to a light simmer.
3. Stir in the vanilla bean seeds, orange zest, cinnamon sticks, cloves and a pinch of salt, then simmer them for 2 min.
4. Stir in the rice, then put on the lid and cook for 15 min on high pressure.
5. Once the time is up, use the natural method to release the pressure.
6. Discard the cinnamon sticks and orange zest strips.
7. Stir the condensed milk into the rice, then serve your pudding warm and enjoy.

   Serve your pudding with some of your favorite fruits diced and enjoy.

APPLE BREAD PUDDING (VEGETARIAN)

The beauty of this recipe is in its simplicity. Enjoy a generous serving of this family friendly dessert in less than half an hour.

Serves: 6 to 8 | Prep Time: 10 mins | Cooking Time: 20 mins

INGREDIENTS

- 2 cans of cinnamon rolls, quartered
- 3 green apples, peeled and finely chopped
- ¾ cup of granulated sugar
- ½ cup of butter, melted
- 1 ½ teaspoon of cinnamon powder

DIRECTIONS

1. Mix the cinnamon and sugar in a small bowl and set it aside.
2. Toss the sugar mix, apple, cinnamon rolls and butter in a large mixing bowl.
3. Pour 1 cup of water into an Instant Pot then place a trivet into it.
4. Transfer the apple mix to a greased baking pan, then place on the trivet.
5. Put on the lid and cook for 20 min on high pressure.
6. Once the time is up, use the natural method to release the pressure.
7. Serve your apple bread pudding and enjoy.

    If you don't like yogurt, ice cream tastes amazing with this recipe.

CHOCOLATE CHIP CAKE (VEGETARIAN)

Chocolate chips with apples? Yup! Two of my favorite ingredients in one cake. Add some salted caramel and let's get this party started!

Serves: 6 to 8 | Prep Time: 15 mins | Cooking Time: 35 mins

INGREDIENTS

- 2 ½ cups of purpose flour
- 2 cups of apple, grated
- 2 cups of sugar, granulated
- 1 cup of walnuts, roughly chopped
- 1 cup of chocolate chips
- 1 cup of butter
- ½ cup of water
- 3 eggs
- 2 tablespoons of cocoa powder
- 1 teaspoon of vanilla extract
- 1 teaspoon of ground allspice
- 1 teaspoon of cinnamon
- 1 teaspoon of baking soda
- Salt

DIRECTIONS

1. Mix together the baking powder, flour, cocoa powder, allspice, cinnamon, baking soda and a pinch of salt in a large mixing bowl.
2. Beat the eggs, butter, sugar, apple, water and vanilla in a large mixing bowl until smooth and creamy.
3. Add the flour mix and whisk until no lumpiness remains.
4. Fold in the walnuts and chocolate chips, then pour the batter into a greased baking pan.
5. Pour 1 cup of water into an Instant Pot, then lower a trivet into it.
6. Cover the cake pan with a piece of foil then place on the trivet.
7. Put on the lid and cook the cake for 35 min on high pressure.
8. Once the time is up, use the natural method to release the pressure.
9. Remove the cake from the pot, discard the piece of foil, and then set it aside to cool down completely.
10. Serve your cake and enjoy.

Sauté some apple slices in butter and sugar until they become soft, then use them to garnish your cake and enjoy.

FESTIVE NUTTY CARROT CAKE (VEGETARIAN)

Holidays are the best, and there is nothing better to remind you of them than a carrot cake with some allspice and nutmeg powder.

Serves: 6 | Prep Time: 10 mins | Cooking Time: 1 hour 14 mins

INGREDIENTS

- 2 carrots, grated
- 2 cups of flour
- 1 ⅓ cups of sugar
- 1 ½ cups of water
- 1 cup of raisins, ground
- 1 cup of walnuts, finely chopped
- 2 tablespoons of butter
- 2 teaspoons of baking soda
- 1 teaspoon of cinnamon powder
- ½ teaspoon of allspice, ground
- ¼ teaspoon of nutmeg powder
- Salt

DIRECTIONS

1. Stir the carrot, cinnamon, butter, nutmeg, allspice, raisins and water in a large saucepan, then bring them to a boil.
2. Boil for 10 min, then turn off the heat and allow them to cool down completely.
3. Add the flour with walnuts, baking soda and a pinch of salt then whisk them until no lumps are found.
4. Pour the batter into a greased baking pan.
5. Pour 1 ½ cups of water into an Instant Pot then lower a trivet into it.
6. Place the cake on the trivet and put on the lid and cook the cake for 1 hour.
7. Once the time is up, use the natural method to release the pressure.
8. Remove the cake from the pot and allow the cake to cool down completely.
9. Serve your cake and enjoy.

Serve your cake with some apricot jam and enjoy.

PINA COLADA PUDDING (VEGETARIAN)

You'll almost be able to feel the sea shore lapping at your feet as you try this pina colada flavored rice pudding. Super delicious!

Serves: 8 | Prep Time: 8 mins | Cooking Time: 12 mins

INGREDIENTS

- 14 ounces of coconut milk
- 1 cup of white rice
- 1 ½ cups of water
- ½ cup of sugar, granulated
- ½ cup of milk
- 2 eggs
- 1 tablespoon of coconut oil
- 1 teaspoon of vanilla extract
- Salt

DIRECTIONS

1. Stir the rice, coconut oil, water and a pinch of salt into an Instant Pot.
2. Put on the lid and cook for 5 min on high pressure.
3. Once the time is up, use the natural method to release the pressure.
4. Beat the eggs, vanilla and milk in a small bowl until smooth.
5. Stir the coconut milk and sugar into the rice, then add the egg mix gradually while stirring all the time.
6. Press the sauté button and bring the pudding to a boil, stirring until it thickens.
7. Serve your pina colada pudding warm and enjoy.

   Serve your pudding with some freshly cut up fruits and whipping cream.

HALLOWEEN STICKY PUDDING (VEGETARIAN)

Don't you just love sticky pudding with caramel sauce and ice cream? My mouth is watering already. What about you?

Serves: 6 | Prep Time: 10 mins | Cooking Time: 3 hours

INGREDIENTS

- 1 ¼ cups of whole wheat flour
- 1 cup of water
- ¾ cup of hot water
- ½ cup of molasses
- ¼ cup of granulated sugar
- ¼ cup of butter, softened
- ¼ cup of butter, melted
- 6 tablespoons of brown sugar
- 1 egg
- 1 teaspoon of vanilla extract
- ¾ teaspoon of baking powder
- ½ teaspoon of ground ginger
- ½ teaspoon of cinnamon
- ⅛ teaspoon of nutmeg powder
- Salt

DIRECTIONS

1. Beat the softened butter and sugar in a large mixing bowl until light and fluffy.
2. Gradually add the egg, followed by vanilla, molasses and cold water, beating all the time.
3. Mix the flour, baking powder, ginger, cinnamon, nutmeg powder, and a pinch of salt in a mixing bowl.
4. Add the flour mix to the butter mix, then mix together until smooth.
5. Sprinkle the brown sugar over the pudding batter.
6. Whisk the hot water and butter in a small bowl, and drizzle over the brown sugar.
7. Pour 1 cup of water into an Instant Pot, then lower a trivet into it.
8. Place the pudding baking pan on the trivet, then put on the lid and cook it for 2 hours 30 min to 3 hours on high.
9. Once the time is up, use the natural method to release the pressure.
10. Serve your pudding warm and enjoy.

Serve your ginger pudding with whipped cream or vanilla ice cream and enjoy.

Maple Stuffed Peaches (Vegetarian)

This dessert is fancy yet deceptively quick; you can cook it in literally three minutes! Isn't that amazing? Serve warm with some ice cream and impress your guests.

Serves: 5 | Prep Time: 10 mins | Cooking Time: 3 mins

INGREDIENTS

- 5 peaches, pitted and holed
- ¼ cup of maple sugar
- ¼ cup of cassava flour
- 2 tablespoons of butter
- ½ teaspoon of cinnamon powder
- ¼ teaspoon of almond extract
- Salt

DIRECTIONS

1. Remove enough peach flesh from the center of each peach to leave only about ½ inch of it left around the edge.

2. Mix the cassava flour, butter, sugar, cinnamon, almond extract and a pinch of salt in a small mixing bowl to make the stuffing.

3. Spoon the filling into the peaches, and stuff them with it.

4. Pour 1 cup of water into an Instant Pot, then lower a trivet into it.

5. Place the stuffed peaches on the trivet, then put on the lid and cook them for 3 min on high pressure.

6. Once the time is up, use the natural method to release the pressure.

7. Allow the stuffed peaches to cool down for 10 min then serve them and enjoy.

    Serve your stuffed peaches with some vanilla yogurt or ice cream and enjoy.

STEAMED LIME BREAD (VEGETARIAN)

Banana bread with a hint of lime is all you need for an incredible dessert (or breakfast!)
that will put a smile on everyone's face.

Serves: 6 | Prep Time: 10 mins | Cooking Time: 20 mins

INGREDIENTS

- 3 cups of stale bread, diced
- 1 cup of sour cream
- 1 cup of almond milk
- 1 cup of ripe banana, sliced
- 1 cup of coconut flakes, toasted
- ½ cup of cane sugar
- 3 egg yolks
- 1 egg
- The zest of 1 lime, grated
- 1 tablespoon of granulated sugar
- 1 teaspoon of vanilla extract
- Salt

DIRECTIONS

1. Beat the egg, sour cream and egg yolks in a large mixing bowl, then beat them until they become smooth.
2. Add the lime zest, vanilla, cane sugar, milk and a pinch of salt, then beat again until smooth.
3. Fold in the banana, bread and coconut flakes, then let them sit for 1 hour.
4. Cover the base of a baking dish, then pour the pudding into it.
5. Tightly cover the pudding dish with another piece of foil.
6. Place the pudding dish in an Instant Pot, and pour enough water into it to cover a third of the pudding dish.
7. Put on the lid and cook the pudding for 20 min on high pressure.
8. Once the time is up, use the natural method to release the pressure.
9. Remove the pudding dish from the pot and discard the foil, then sprinkle the sugar over it.
10. Broil the pudding in the oven for 5 min, then serve and enjoy.

    Serve your bread pudding with some ice cream and enjoy.

FESTIVE SWEET BUTTERMILK CAKE (VEGETARIAN)

Sweet potato plays an unlikely starring role in this delicious cake that is only a little frosting away from making a perfect Christmas treat!
Serves: 8 | Prep Time: 10 mins | Cooking Time: 1 hour 10 mins

INGREDIENTS

- 1 ¾ cups of purpose flour
- 1 cup of sweet potato, cooked and mashed
- 1 cup of granulated sugar
- ¾ cup of raisins
- ¾ cup of walnuts, finely chopped
- ½ cup of oil
- ½ cup of brown sugar
- ⅓ cup of buttermilk
- 2 eggs
- 1 teaspoon of baking soda
- 1 teaspoon of ground cloves
- 1 teaspoon of cinnamon
- 1 teaspoon of nutmeg powder
- Salt

DIRECTIONS

1. Beat the eggs, buttermilk, and brown and granulated sugar in a large mixing bowl until smooth.
2. Mix the cloves, flour, cinnamon, nutmeg powder, baking soda and a pinch of salt in a small bowl.
3. Add the flour mix to the egg mix, and whisk until all lumpiness is gone.
4. Gently fold the walnuts, raisins and sweet potato into the batter.
5. Pour half of the cake batter into a greased baking pan, and cover with a piece of foil.
6. Pour 1 cup of water into an Instant Pot and lower into a trivet.
7. Place the cake pan on the trivet, then put on the lid and cook for 35 min on high pressure.
8. Once the time is up, use the natural method to release the pressure.
9. Place the cake on a rack to cool down completely, then repeat the process with the remaining batter to make a second cake.
    Serve your cake with your favorite frosting and enjoy.

TOOTHY-FRUITY CAKE (VEGETARIAN)

This candied fruit and nut cake is the perfect showpiece to wow friends and family with your skills.

Serves: 6 | Prep Time: 15 mins | Cooking Time: 1 hour 33 mins

INGREDIENTS

- 1 cup of purpose flour
- ¾ cup of brown sugar
- 2 eggs, beaten
- 6 tablespoons of butter, softened
- 1 tablespoon of orange zest, grated
- 1 teaspoon of baking powder
- 1 teaspoon of vanilla extract
- ½ teaspoon of cinnamon powder
- ½ cup of bourbon
- ¼ cup of pecans, finely chopped
- ¼ cup of almonds, finely chopped
- ¼ cup of hazelnuts, finely chopped
- ¼ cup of pistachios, finely chopped
- ¼ cup of walnuts, finely chopped
- ¼ cup of candied cherries
- ¼ cup of candied apples
- ¼ cup of candied pineapple
- ¼ cup of dehydrated grapes
- Salt

DIRECTIONS

1. Pour the bourbon into a small saucepan and bring it to a simmer.
2. Place the candied apples, cherries, pineapple and grapes into a mixing bowl, then pour the bourbon over them and set aside.
3. Beat the brown sugar and butter in a large mixing bowl until light and fluffy.
4. Gradually add the eggs, followed by the vanilla, orange zest and cinnamon, beating all the time until the mix becomes smooth.
5. Mix the baking soda and flour in a small bowl, then add to the batter, whisking all lumpiness is gone.
6. Fold in the candied fruit mix and chopped nuts, then pour the batter into a greased baking pan.
7. Pour 1 ½ cups of water into an Instant Pot then lower into it a trivet.
8. Place the cake pan on the trivet and put on the lid then cook the cake for 1 hour 30 min on high pressure.
9. Once the time is up, use the natural method to release the pressure.
10. Remove the cake from the pot and allow to cool down completely, then serve it and enjoy.

Serve your cake with ice cream and enjoy. You can also try it with jam as a breakfast option.

CARDAMOM PEAR CAKE (VEGETARIAN)

If you are looking for a delicious vegan cake, either for yourself or your awkward vegan friend, fret no more! This scrumptious pear cake will floor everybody who tastes it.

Serves: 4 to 6 | Prep Time: 10 mins | Cooking Time: 35 mins

INGREDIENTS

- 1 ¼ cups of whole wheat pastry flour
- 1 cup of fresh pears, finely chopped
- ½ cup of milk
- ½ cup of cranberries
- ¼ cup of sugar
- 2 tablespoons of applesauce
- 2 tablespoons of ground flax seeds
- ½ teaspoon of baking soda
- ½ teaspoon of baking powder
- ½ teaspoon of ground cardamom
- Salt

DIRECTIONS

1. Mix the flour, sugar, baking soda and powder, cardamom, and a pinch of salt in a large mixing bowl.
2. Whisk the flax seed, milk and applesauce in a large mixing bowl until they are combined.
3. Add the flour mix, and whisk until no lumps are found.
4. Fold in the chopped pear with cranberries then pour the batter into a greased baking pan.
5. Pour 1 ½ cups of water into an Instant Pot then lower a trivet into it.
6. Place the cake pan on the trivet, and put on the lid then cook the cake for 35 min on high pressure.
7. Once the time is up, use the natural method to release the pressure.
8. Remove the cake from the pot, allow it to cool down completely, then serve it and enjoy.

Garnish your cake with some extra fresh cranberries and whipped toppings, and enjoy.

LEMONGRASS PUDDING (VEGETARIAN)

Who said lemongrass can only be used in savory dishes? This recipe is evidence that lemongrass is a very versatile ingredient that can lend its unique taste to desserts, too.

Serves: 8 | Prep Time: 8 mins | Cooking Time: 6 mins

INGREDIENTS

- 4 cups of coconut milk beverage
- 1 cup of pearl tapioca
- 1 cup of sugar
- 1 cup of coconut milk
- 4 egg yolks
- 6 inches of fresh lemongrass, crushed
- 2 teaspoons of fresh ginger, minced
- Salt

DIRECTIONS

1. Stir the lemongrass, coconut milk beverage, ginger and tapioca into an Instant Pot.
2. Put on the lid and cook for 6 min on high pressure.
3. Once the time is up, use the natural method to release the pressure.
4. Whisk the egg yolks, coconut milk, sugar and a pinch of salt in a mixing bowl.
5. Add the egg mix to the tapioca pudding, and stir completely.
6. Press the sauté button on the pot, and bring to a boil.
7. Spoon the pudding into serving glasses, and allow them to cool down completely.
8. Serve your pudding and enjoy.

Top your pudding with mixed chopped nuts and fruits, then serve it and enjoy.

BUTTERMILK BANANA BAKE (VEGETARIAN)

This buttermilk and banana bread cake makes a delicious dessert as well breakfast, if you happen to have leftovers. Serve with butter or jelly and eat like a champion.

Serves: 8 | Prep Time: 10 mins | Cooking Time: 55 mins

INGREDIENTS

- 3 ripe bananas, cut into chunks
- 1 ¾ cups of purpose flour
- 1 cup of white sugar
- ½ cup of butter
- ¼ cup of buttermilk
- ¼ cup of butter
- 2 eggs
- 1 egg white
- 1 ½ teaspoons of baking powder
- ½ teaspoon of vanilla extract
- ½ teaspoon of baking soda
- Salt

DIRECTIONS

1. Beat the white and brown sugar and butter in a large mixing bowl until light and fluffy.
2. Gradually add the bananas followed by eggs, buttermilk and vanilla, beating all the time until smooth.
3. Mix the flour, baking powder, baking soda and a pinch of salt in a mixing bowl, then add to the egg mix and whisk until no lumpiness remains.
4. Pour the batter into a greased baking pan, and cover with a piece of foil.
5. Pour 1 ½ cups of water into an Instant Pot, then lower a trivet into it, and place the cake pan on the trivet.
6. Put on the lid and cook the cake for 55 min on high pressure.
7. Once the time is up, use the natural method to release the pressure.
8. Remove the cake from the pot and discard the piece of foil then set it aside to cool down completely.
9. Serve your cake and enjoy.

Some vegan butter or jam with this banana bread will go down a treat the morning after!

BACON PUDDING

Bacon? For dessert? Are you for real? These questions might be running through your mind as you read through this recipe, but if you try it, you won't be able to open your mouth to ask because you'll be too busy chomping and enjoying life!

Serves: 4 | Prep Time: 10 mins | Cooking Time: 22 mins

INGREDIENTS

- 6 thick (¼-inch) slices of white bread, diced
- 1 ½ cups of milk
- 6 bacon slices
- 3 eggs
- 2 tablespoons of maple syrup
- ¼ teaspoon of nutmeg powder
- Salt

DIRECTIONS

1. Cook the bacon slices in a large skillet until crisp.
2. Drain the bacon slices and finely chop them, then toss them in a mixing bowl with the diced bread.
3. Whisk the eggs with milk, nutmeg powder, maple syrup and a pinch of salt in a large mixing bowl.
4. Stir in the bread mix then transfer them into a greased baking dish.
5. Cover the dish with a piece of foil then let sit for 10 min.
6. Pour 1 ½ cups of water into an Instant Pot then lower into it a trivet and place the baking dish on it.
7. Put on the lid and cook the pudding for 18 min on high pressure.
8. Once the time is up, use the natural method to release the pressure.
9. Serve your pudding warm and enjoy.

    Serve your pudding with some extra maple syrup and enjoy.

Classic Coconut Pudding (Vegan)

10 minutes is all you need for a classic and easy rice pudding that you can serve at any time of day. What's even better is that most of the ingredients you need for it are already sitting in your kitchen cupboards.

Serves: 4 | Prep Time: 5 mins | Cooking Time: 5 mins

INGREDIENTS

- 2 cups of vanilla almond milk
- 1 cup of aborio rice
- 1 cup of coconut milk
- ⅓ cup of coconut sugar
- 1 tablespoon of cocoa powder
- 2 teaspoons of vanilla extract
- Salt

DIRECTIONS

1. Stir the almond and coconut milk in an Instant Pot.
2. Press the sauté button on the pot and bring to a boil.
3. Stir in the rice with a pinch of salt, then put on the lid and cook for 5 min on high pressure.
4. Once the time is up, use the natural method to release the pressure.
5. Stir in the cocoa powder with vanilla extract.
6. Serve your pudding warm and enjoy.

   Serve this simple treat with some chopped almonds and enjoy.

CHERRY PIE (VEGETARIAN)

I first enjoyed this delicious cherry pie on Valentine's Day and it has ever since held some romantic connotations. At the very least, you'll be falling in love with the recipe!

Serves: 4 to 6 | Prep Time: 10 mins | Cooking Time: 15 mins

INGREDIENTS

- 9 inches double pie crust
- 4 cups of tart cherries, pitted
- 1 cup of white sugar
- 4 tablespoons of quick cooking tapioca
- 1 ½ tablespoons of butter
- ½ teaspoon of vanilla extract
- ¼ teaspoon of almond extract
- Salt

DIRECTIONS

1. Mix the cherries, sugar, vanilla, almond, tapioca and a pinch of salt in a mixing bowl to make the filling.
2. Let the filling stand for 15 min.
3. Place the bottom of the crust into the bottom of a greased baking pan, then pour the filling into it.
4. Place the butter in the shape of dots on the filling.
5. Cover the filling with the upper crust, then create several holes in it with a fork.
6. Pour 2 cups of water into an Instant Pot then lower a trivet into it.
7. Place the pie pan on the trivet and put on the lid, then cook it for 15 min on high pressure.
8. Once the time is up, use the natural method to release the pressure.
9. Set the cherry pie aside, and allow it to cool down completely. Serve and enjoy.

Serve your cherry pie with some ice cream and enjoy.

STICKY CARAMEL CAKE (VEGETARIAN)

Doesn't your mouth water instantly just thinking about caramel? That golden sauce that makes absolutely anything delicious is doing the same thing for this cake in the form of candies. Added to peanut butter, it's a dream come true.

Serves: 8 | Prep Time: 10 mins | Cooking Time: 3 hours

INGREDIENTS

- 1 cup of purpose flour
- 1 cup of boiling water
- 1 cup of granulated sugar, divided
- 1 cup of milk
- ¾ cup of peanut butter
- ⅓ cup of vegetable oil
- 18 caramel candy, unwrapped
- 3 tablespoons of cocoa powder
- 1 teaspoon of baking powder
- Salt

DIRECTIONS

1. Mix the baking powder, flour, ½ cup of sugar and a pinch of salt in a large mixing bowl.
2. Add the vanilla, oil, peanut butter and milk, then whisk until smooth.
3. Spread half of the batter into a greased baking pan, then top with the caramel candy followed by the remaining batter.
4. Whisk the remaining sugar, cocoa powder and boiling water in a small bowl until all lumpiness is gone.
5. Drizzle the water mix over them.
6. Pour 2 cups of water into an Instant Pot, then lower a trivet into it.
7. Place the cake pan on the trivet and put on the lid. Cook the cake for 2 to 3 hours on high by using the slow cooking feature.
8. Once the time is up, use the natural method to release the pressure.
9. Remove the cake from the pot and allow to cool down completely, then serve warm and enjoy.

   Serve your cake with some extra caramel sauce and ice cream and enjoy.

VANILLA BUTTERSCOTCH (VEGETARIAN)

This tasty butterscotch with fruit slices makes a sweet aphrodisiac that you will keep coming back to time and time again.

Serves: 5 ¼ cups | Prep Time: 5 mins | Cooking Time: 3 hours

INGREDIENTS

- 28 ounces of condensed milk, sweetened
- 2 cups of brown sugar
- 1 cup of butter, melted
- ⅔ cup of light corn syrup
- ¼ cup of milk
- 1 teaspoon of vanilla extract
- Salt

DIRECTIONS

1. Stir the vanilla, butter, condensed milk, sugar, corn syrup and a pinch of salt into an Instant Pot.
2. Put on the lid and cook the fondue for 3 hours on low.
3. Once the time is up, use the natural method to release the pressure.
4. Add the milk gradually while whisking all the time until smooth.
5. Serve your butterscotch fondue warm and enjoy.

Serve your fondue with some fresh fruit slices.

Classic Messy Coconut Cake (Vegetarian)

When you open the pot, this cake will look a total mess; but once you serve it up with ice cream and caramel sauce, it will look a hot mess instead!

Serves: 8 | Prep Time: 10 mins | Cooking Time: 3 hours

Ingredients

- 1 package of moist white cake mix
- 28 ounces of coconut milk
- 3 ½ ounces of coconut flakes
- 1 cup of butter, diced
- Salt

Directions

1. Stir the white cake mix, and coconut milk and flakes, into an Instant Pot.
2. Place the diced butter on top, then put on the lid and cook the cake for 2 hours on high by using the slow cook feature.
3. Once the time is up, use the quick method to release the pressure.
4. Stir quickly and scrape the sides, then put on the lid and cook it for 1 hour on high.
5. Serve your cake warm and enjoy.

   Serve your coconut cake with some vanilla bean ice cream and enjoy.

APPLE PEACH COBBLER (VEGETARIAN)

In smoothies, juices and savory dishes, peaches are always the best; and in this cobbler, they are totally rocking it! The crumbly texture of the crust in contrast with the soft peaches is just perfect.

Serves: 8 | Prep Time: 10 mins | Cooking Time: 6 to 9 hours

INGREDIENTS

- 3 pounds of peach, sliced
- 1 ½ cups of purpose flour
- 1 ¼ cups of milk
- 1 cup of granulated sugar, divided
- ¾ cup of cornmeal
- ¾ cup of apple butter
- ½ cup of butter, melted
- ¼ cup of bourbon
- Salt

DIRECTIONS

1. To make the filling, toss ¼ cup of sugar, peach, bourbon, apple butter and a pinch of salt in a large mixing bowl.
2. Spread the filling in the bottom of a greased Instant Pot.
3. Mix the flour with ¾ cup of sugar, cornmeal and a pinch of salt in a large mixing bowl.
4. Add the milk, gradually followed by the melted butter, mixing all the time.
5. Spread the flour mix all over the peach filling.
6. Put on the lid and cook the cobbler for 4 to 6 hours on high or 8 to 9 hours on low.
7. Once the time is up, use the natural method to release the pressure.
8. Serve your cobbler warm and enjoy.

Serve your cobbler with some ice cream and enjoy.

CARAMEL MACCHIATO CAKE (VEGETARIAN)

Caramel macchiato is a delicious drink, but did you know it also comes in cake form? This is the perfect after party treat to wow your guests.

Serves: 8 | Prep Time: 10 mins | Cooking Time: 2 hours 30 min

INGREDIENTS

- 15 ounces of yellow cake mix
- 1 ½ cups of boiling water
- 1 cup of international delight mix (caramel macchiato)
- ¾ cup of brown sugar
- 3 eggs
- ½ cup of vegetable oil
- 2 tablespoons of butter
- Salt

DIRECTIONS

1. Combine the oil with cake mix, caramel macchiato and eggs in a large mixing bowl, then mix them until they become smooth.
2. Pour the batter into a greased Instant Pot.
3. Whisk the boiling water with sugar and butter in a small bowl, then sprinkle the mix on top of the cake batter.
4. Cover the pot with a paper towel, then put on the lid and cook the cake for 1 hours 30 min to 2 hours 30 min on high, or until it is done.
5. Once the time is up, use the natural method to release the pressure.
6. Remove the cake from the pot and allow it to cool down slightly.
7. Serve your cake warm with some caramel sauce and ice cream, and enjoy.

   If you don't want or like yogurt, ice cream tastes amazing with this recipe.

LEMON CHEESECAKE (VEGAN)

Yes, traditional cheesecake is good, but this vegan cheesecake gives it a run for its money. The taste and texture of the crust and filling are like ice and fire, an unimaginable taste that needs to be tried to be believed.

Serves: 8 | Prep Time: 15 mins | Cooking Time: 20 mins

INGREDIENTS

- 1 cup of cashews, soaked for 30 min
- 1 cup of quick oats
- ½ cup of dates, soaked for 30 min
- ½ cup of walnuts, finely chopped
- ½ cup of coconut flour
- ½ cup of vanilla almond milk
- ¼ cup of coconut palm sugar
- 2 teaspoons of lemon zest, grated
- 2 tablespoons of fresh lemon juice
- 1 tablespoon of arrowroot powder
- 1 teaspoon of vanilla extract
- Salt

DIRECTIONS

1. Soak the cashews and dates in two different bowls with ¼ cup of water for 15 to 30 min.
2. Transfer the soaked dates, oats and walnuts to a food processor, and blend smooth. Add some water if the mix is too dry.
3. Press the crust mix to the bottom of a greased baking pan, then set aside.
4. Drain the cashews and transfer to a food processor with half of their soaking water. Blend until smooth.
5. Add the lemon juice, sugar, coconut flour, milk, lemon zest, vanilla extract and a pinch of salt, then blend until smooth to make the filling.
6. Add the arrowroot powder and blend until smooth again.
7. Pour the filling into the crust then cover the pan with a piece of foil.
8. Pour 2 cups of water into an Instant Pot, then lower a trivet into it.
9. Place the cheesecake on the trivet, put on the lid, and cook for 20 min on high pressure.
10. Once the time is up, use the natural method to release the pressure.
11. Remove the cheesecake from the pot and let it sit for 30 min.
12. Refrigerate the cake for 3 to 4 hours, and then serve and enjoy.

Garnish your cake with some fresh berries and enjoy.

Turtle Pull-Apart Biscuits (Vegetarian)

Almost everybody loves biscuits, and they are the heart of this delicious pull-apart treat that will go down a treat after dinner.

Serves: 8 | Prep Time: 10 mins | Cooking Time: 2 hours

INGREDIENTS

- 16 ounces of refrigerated buttermilk biscuits, quartered
- ⅔ cup of brown sugar
- ⅔ cup of pecan halves
- ½ cup of butter, melted
- ⅓ cup of chocolate chips
- ¼ cup of granulated sugar
- 2 tablespoons of whipping cream
- Salt

DIRECTIONS

1. Stir the butter and brown sugar in a small heavy pan over low heat until they completely melt.
2. Place the granulated sugar in a large zip-lock bag, then toss in the biscuit quarters in batches.
3. Lay ¼ cup of pecans in the bottom of a greased Instant Pot then top it with ⅓ of the biscuits followed by ⅓ of the butter mix.
4. Repeat the process to make another 3 layers, with the pecans on top.
5. Put on the lid and cook for 1 hour 30 min to 2 hours on high by using the slow cooker feature.
6. Once the time is up, use the natural method to release the pressure.
7. Pour the heavy cream into a small saucepan and bring to the boil.
8. Turn off the heat and stir in the chocolate chips until completely melted to make the sauce.
9. Drizzle the chocolate sauce all over the biscuit turtle.
10. Serve your biscuit turtle warm and enjoy.

Serve with some caramel sauce and enjoy.

32

CHOCOLATE FUDGE CAKE (VEGAN)

I love traditional fudge squares, but this chocolate fudge cake is a whole other level. Serve with ice cream on a hot summer night and you have perfection!

Serves: 8 | Prep Time: 10 mins | Cooking Time: 2 hours to 2 hours 30 mins

INGREDIENTS

- 1 cup of purpose flour
- ½ cup of granulated sugar
- ½ cup of chocolate almond milk
- 2 tablespoons of canola oil
- 2 tablespoons of dark cocoa powder
- 2 teaspoons of baking powder
- 1 teaspoon of vanilla extract
- Salt

DIRECTIONS

1. Mix the baking powder, flour, sugar, cocoa powder and a pinch of salt in a large mixing bowl.
2. Add the oil, almond milk and vanilla extract, then whisk until smooth.
3. Pour the batter into a greased Instant Pot.
4. Put on the lid, and cook the cake on high for 2 hours to 2 hours 30 min by using the slow cooking feature.
5. Once the time is up, use the natural method to release the pressure.
6. Remove the lid and allow the cake to cool down completely. Serve and enjoy.

    Garnish your cake with some chocolate sauce and whipped cream.

GENERAL COOKING TIMES

The wonderful folk behind the Instant Pot have put together some typical cooking times for common food items. All cooking times are approximate. Please use them as a guideline only. Here they are for your reference:

NB: If you're reading this on a Kindle or other e-reader, you may find the paperback version better for reading the tables!

BEANS, LEGUMES & LENTILS

Dried beans double in volume and weight after soaking or cooking. To avoid overflow in the inner pot, do not fill it more than ½ full.

When cooking dried beans, use enough liquid to cover the beans

Although not strictly necessary, soaking dried beans can speed up cooking.

Beans and legumes are less prone to be over-cooked. But if they are undercooked, the texture is quite hard and unpleasant. So consider the cooking time as minimal time. Letting the cooker cool naturally is the best way to save energy and achieve best results.

NB: Cooking time is pressure cooking time on Instant Pot or other electric pressure cooker operating at 10.2 – 11.6 psi or 70-80 kPa.

Dried Beans & Legume	Dry, Cooking Time (in Minutes)	Soaked, Cooking Time (in Minutes)
Adzuki	20 – 25	10 – 15
Anasazi	20 – 25	10 – 15
Black beans	20 – 25	10 – 15
Black-eyed peas	20 – 25	10 – 15
Chickpeas (chick peas, garbanzo bean or kabuli)	35 – 40	20 – 25
Cannellini beans	35 – 40	20 – 25
Gandules (pigeon peas)	20 – 25	15 – 20
Great Northern beans	25 – 30	20 – 25
Lentils, French green	15 – 20	N/A

Lentils, green, mini (brown)	15 – 20	N/A
Lentils, red, split	15 – 18	N/A
Lentils, yellow, split (moong dal)	15 – 18	N/A
Lima beans	20 – 25	10 – 15
Kidney beans, red	25 – 30	20 – 25
Kidney beans, white	35 – 40	20 – 25
Navy beans	25 – 30	20 – 25
Pinto beans	25 – 30	20 – 25
Peas	15 – 20	10 – 15
Scarlet runner	20 – 25	10 – 15
Soy beans	25 – 30	20 – 25

Raw meat is a perishable food that should not be left at room temperature for more than 2 hours (or 1 hour if room temperature is above 32C/180F). When using delayed cooking start, do not set delayed start for more than 1 ~ 2 hours. It is recommended to cook the meat first and use the automatic Keep-warm function to maintain the food at serving temperature.

Do not try to thicken sauce before cooking. Corn starch, flour or arrow-root may deposit to the bottom of the inner pot and be burnt on the base and so block heat dissipation. This could cause overheating or cut out.

You may want to brown the meat to seal the natural juices before commencing pressure cooking.

NB: Cooking time is pressure cooking time on Instant Pot or other electric pressure cooker operating at 10.2 – 11.6 psi or 70-80 kPa.

Meat	Cooking Time (in Minutes)
Beef, stew meat	15 – 20
Beef, meat ball	Oct-15
Beef, dressed	20 – 25
Beef, pot roast, steak, rump, round, chuck, blade or brisket, large	35 – 40
Beef, pot roast, steak, rump, round, chuck, blade or brisket, small chunks	25 – 30
Beef, ribs	25 – 30
Beef, shanks	25 – 30
Beef, oxtail	40 – 50
Chicken, breasts	8 – 10
Chicken, whole	20 – 25
Chicken, cut up with bones	10 – 15

Chicken, drumsticks, legs or thighs	10 – 15
Cornish Hen, whole	10 – 15
Duck, cut up with bones	10 – 12
Duck, whole	25 – 30
Ham slice	9 – 12
Ham shoulder	25 – 30
Lamb, cubes,	Oct-15
Lamb, stew meat	Oct-15
Lamb, leg	35 – 45
Pheasant	20 – 25
Pork, loin roast	55 – 60
Pork, butt roast	45 – 50
Pork, ribs	20 – 25
Turkey, breast, boneless	15 – 20
Turkey, breast, whole, with bones	25 – 30
Turkey, drumsticks (leg)	15 – 20
Veal, chops	5 – 8
Veal, roast	35 – 45
Quail, whole	8 – 10

SEAFOOD & FISH

When steaming seafood & fish, you need at least 1 cup of water (250ml), an ovenproof or steel bowl on a trivet. When seafood is over-cooked, the texture turns tough. Unless that's intended, you should control cooking time precisely.

Normally, you need to use the steam release to release pressure and stop cooking, as soon as the cooking period is over. An alternative is to take natural cooling time (7~10 minutes) into consideration.

Please note that the cooking time is pressure cooking time on Instant Pot or other electric pressure cooker operating at $10.2 - 11.6$ psi or 70-80 kPa.

Seafood and Fish	Fresh, Cooking Time (in Minutes)	Frozen, Cooking Time (in Minutes)
Crab	3 – 4	5 – 6
Fish, whole (trout, snapper, etc.)	5 – 6	7 – 10
Fish fillet,	2 – 3	3 – 4
Fish steak	3 – 4	4 – 6
Lobster	3 – 4	4 – 6
Mussels	2 – 3	4 – 5
Seafood soup or stock	6 – 7	7 – 9
Shrimp or Prawn	1 – 2	2 – 3

When steaming veg, you need at least 1 cup of water (250ml), plus ovenproof or steel bowl on a trivet. Due to short pressure cooking time, leaving the cooker to naturally cool down without using the steam release will add extra cooking time.

NB: Cooking time is pressure cooking time on Instant Pot or other electric pressure cookers operating at the preset pressure level.

The cooking time is for small or medium amount. For large amount, add more water and increase the time by 20~40%.

Vegetable	Fresh, Cooking Time (in Minutes)	Frozen, Cooking Time (in Minutes)
Artichoke, whole, trimmed without leaves	9 – 11	11 – 13
Artichoke, hearts	4 – 5	5 – 6
Asparagus, whole or cut	1 – 2	2 – 3
Beans, green/yellow or wax, whole, trim ends and strings	1 – 2	2 – 3
Beets, small roots, whole	11 – 13	13 – 15
Beetroot, large roots, whole	20 – 25	25 – 30
Broccoli, florets	2 – 3	3 – 4
Broccoli, stalks	3 – 4	4 – 5
Brussel sprouts, whole	3 – 4	4 – 5
Cabbage, red, purple or green, shredded	2 – 3	3 – 4
Cabbage, red, purple or green, wedges	3 – 4	4 – 5

Carrots, sliced or shredded	1 − 2	2 − 3
Carrots, whole or chunked	2 − 3	3 − 4
Cauliflower florets	2 − 3	3 − 4
Celery, chunks	2 − 3	3 − 4
Collard	4 − 5	5 − 6
Corn, kernels	1 − 2	2 − 3
Corn, on the cob	3 − 4	4 − 5
Aubergine, slices or chunks	2 − 3	3 − 4
Endive	1 − 2	2 − 3
Escarole, chopped	1 − 2	2 − 3
Green beans, whole	2 − 3	3 − 4
Greens (beetroot greens, collards, kale, spinach, swiss chard, turnip greens), chopped	3 − 6	4 − 7
Leeks	2 − 4	3 − 5
Mixed vegetables	2 − 3	3 − 4
Okra	2 − 3	3 − 4

Onions, sliced	2 – 3	3 – 4
Parsnips, sliced	1 – 2	2 – 3
Parsnips, chunks	2 – 4	4 – 6
Peas, in the pod	1 – 2	2 – 3
Peas, green	1 – 2	2 – 3
Potatoes, in cubes	7 – 9	9 – 11
Potatoes, whole, baby	10 – 12	12 – 14
Potatoes, whole, large	12 – 15	15 – 19
Pumpkin, small slices or chunks	4 – 5	6 – 7
Pumpkin, large slices or chunks	8 – 10	10 – 14
Rutabaga, slices	3 – 5	4 – 6
Rutabaga, chunks	4 – 6	6 – 8
Spinach	1 – 2	3 – 4
Squash, acorn, slices or chunks	6 – 7	8 – 9
Squash, butternut, slices or chunks	8 – 10	10 – 12
Sweet potato, in cubes	7 – 9	9 – 11

Sweet potato, whole, small	10 – 12	12 – 14
Sweet potato, whole, large	12 – 15	15 – 19
Sweet pepper, slices or chunks	1 – 3	2 – 4
Tomatoes, in quarters	2 – 3	4 – 5
Tomatoes, whole	3 – 5	5 – 7
Turnip, chunks	2 – 4	4 – 6
Yam, in cubes	7 – 9	9 – 11
Yam, whole, small	10 – 12	12 – 14
Yam, whole, large	12 – 15	15 – 19
Zucchini (Courgette), slices or chunks	2 – 3	3 – 4

RICE & GRAINS

Instant Pot's built-in "Rice" and "Multigrain" function keys normally provide the best way to cook rice and grains. The marks on the inner pot are a general guideline on total amount of grain + water. If you want to cook specialty rice or grains, use the following grain:water ratio.

The measuring cup provided (180ml) can be used to measure the grain-water ratios. 1 cup of grain yields about one adult serving.

NB: Cooking time is pressure cooking time for Instant Pot or other electric pressure cooker operating at 10.2 − 11.6 psi or 70-80 kPa.

Rice & Grain	Water Quantity Grain : Water ratios)	Cooking Time (in Minutes)
Barley, pearl	01:04	25 – 30
Barley, pot	1:3 ~ 1:4	25 – 30
Congee, thick	1:4 ~ 1:5	15 – 20
Congee, thin	1:6 ~ 1:7	15 – 20
Couscous	01:02	5 – 8
Corn, dried, half	01:03	25 – 30
Kamut, whole	01:03	10 – 12
Millet	02/03/17 01:01	10 – 12
Oats, quick cooking	02/03/17 01:01	6
Oats, steel-cut	02/03/17 01:01	10

Porridge, thin	1:6 ~ 1:7	15 − 20
Quinoa, quick cooking	01:02	8
Rice, Basmati	01:01.5	4 − 8
Rice, Brown	01:01.3	22 − 28
Rice, Jasmine	01:01	4 − 10
Rice, white	01:01.5	8
Rice, wild	01:03	25 − 30
Sorghum	01:03	20 − 25
Spelt berries	01:03	15 − 20
Wheat berries	01:03	25 − 30

FRUITS

When steaming fruit you need one cup of water (250ml), an ovenproof or steel bowl on a trivet. Normally fruit dishes have precise requirements for the texture of the fruit so precise timing is essential. Instead of leaving the cooker to naturally cool down, you'll need to use the steam release to release the pressure and stop cooking.

Fruits	Fresh, Cooking Time (in Minutes)	Dried, Cooking Time (in Minutes)
Apples, in slices or pieces	2 – 3	3 – 4
Apples, whole	3 – 4	4 – 6
Apricots, whole or halves	2 – 3	3 – 4
Peaches	2 – 3	4 – 5
Pears, whole	3 – 4	4 – 6
Pears, slices or halves	2 – 3	4 – 5
Prunes	2 – 3	4 – 5
Raisins	N/A	4 – 5

MEASUREMENT CONVERSIONS

All my recipes are presented in US format. I'm not much of a stickler for absolute measurements because cooking is an art, not a science, however I realize some people may find the measurements a little confusing.

For your reference I've included some common conversions from US to metric in the following sections. So now everybody's happy!

LIQUIDS, HERBS & SPICES

Customary Qty	Metric
1 teaspoon	5 mL
1 tablespoon *or* 1/2 fluid ounce	15 mL
1 fluid ounce *or* 1/8 cup	30 mL
1/4 cup *or* 2 fluid ounces	60 mL
1/3 cup	80 mL
1/2 cup *or* 4 fluid ounces	120 mL
2/3 cup	160 mL
3/4 cup *or* 6 fluid ounces	180 mL
1 cup *or* 8 fluid ounces *or* half a pint	240 mL
1 1/2 cups *or* 12 fluid ounces	350 mL
2 cups *or* 1 pint *or* 16 fluid ounces	475 mL
3 cups *or* 1 1/2 pints	700 mL
4 cups *or* 2 pints *or* 1 quart	950 mL
4 quarts *or* 1 gallon	3.8 L
Where precision is not necessary, you may prefer to round these conversions off as below:	
1 cup = 250 mL	
1 pint = 500 mL	
1 quart = 1 L	
1 gallon = 4 L	

WEIGHTS

Customary Qty	Metric
1 ounce	28 g
4 ounces *or* 1/4 pound	113 g
1/3 pound	150 g
8 ounces *or* 1/2 pound	230 g
2/3 pound	300 g
12 ounces *or* 3/4 pound	340 g
1 pound *or* 16 ounces	450 g
2 pounds	900 g

COMMON NON-LIQUIDS BY WEIGHT

Ingredient	1 cup	3/4 cup	2/3 cup	1/2 cup	1/3 cup	1/4 cup	2 Tbsp
Flour, all purpose (wheat)	120 g	90 g	80 g	60 g	40 g	30 g	15 g
Flour, well sifted all purpose (wheat)	110 g	80 g	70 g	55 g	35 g	27 g	13 g
Sugar, granulated cane	200 g	150 g	130 g	100 g	65 g	50 g	25 g
Confectioner's sugar (cane)	100 g	75 g	70 g	50 g	35 g	25 g	13 g
Brown sugar, packed firmly (but not too firmly)	180 g	135 g	120 g	90 g	60 g	45 g	23 g
Corn meal	160 g	120 g	100 g	80 g	50 g	40 g	20 g
Corn starch	120 g	90 g	80 g	60 g	40 g	30 g	15 g
Rice, uncooked	190 g	140 g	125 g	95 g	65 g	48 g	24 g
Macaroni, uncooked	140 g	100 g	90 g	70 g	45 g	35 g	17 g
Couscous, uncooked	180 g	135 g	120 g	90 g	60 g	45 g	22 g
Oats, uncooked quick	90 g	65 g	60 g	45 g	30 g	22 g	11 g
Table salt	300 g	230 g	200 g	150 g	100 g	75 g	40 g
Butter	240 g	180 g	160 g	120 g	80 g	60 g	30 g
Vegetable shortening	190 g	140 g	125 g	95 g	65 g	48 g	24 g
Chopped fruits and vegetables	150 g	110 g	100 g	75 g	50 g	40 g	20 g
Nuts, chopped	150 g	110 g	100 g	75 g	50 g	40 g	20 g
Nuts, ground	120 g	90 g	80 g	60 g	40 g	30 g	15 g
Bread crumbs, fresh, loosely packed	60 g	45 g	40 g	30 g	20 g	15 g	8 g
Bread crumbs, dry	150 g	110 g	100 g	75 g	50 g	40 g	20 g
Parmesan cheese, grated	90 g	65 g	60 g	45 g	30 g	22 g	11 g

Bonus: Get Free Cookbooks Like This One

I'm always cooking, and love sharing my favorite recipes with friends and family. Occasionally I will even give entire cookbooks away for free to help spread the word and try out new ideas.

If you'd like to join my inner circle and receive free cookbooks like this one then click the link below and I'll add you to my super secret list. Whenever I have a freebie available, you'll be the first to know!

• **Visit http://geni.us/cookbookaddicts to join the club!** •

LIKE THIS BOOK?

These handsome scamps love their food just as much as I do! And they love hearing your feedback, too. OK, maybe that's just me.

Nothing makes me happier than hearing about your favorite recipes. If you'd like to share yours, please visit your Amazon purchase history to leave a quick review. I read every single one, and you can even upload a picture of your creations if you're feeling like a super big show-off!

a Review Now!

Visit your Amazon purchase history to share a review ☺

CPSIA information can be obtained
at www.ICGtesting.com
Printed in the USA
LVOW06s0428181217
560134LV00008B/633/P